Felties

How to Make 18 Cute and Fuzzy Friends

Nelly Pailloux

Ivy Press

First published in the UK in 2009 by

Ivy Press
210 High Street, Lewes
East Sussex BN7 2NS, UK
www.ivypress.co.uk

Copyright © Ivy Press Limited 2009

All rights reserved. No part of this book may be reproduced or transmitted in any form or by any means, electronic or mechanical, including photocopying, recording, or by any information storage-and-retrieval system, without written permission from the copyright holder.

British Library Cataloguing-in-Publication Data
A catalogue record for this book is available from the British Library

ISBN: 978-1-905695-87-4

Ivy Press
This book was conceived, designed, and produced by Ivy Press

Creative Director Peter Bridgewater
Publisher Jason Hook
Editorial Director Tom Kitch
Senior Editor Polita Caaveiro
Art Director Wayne Blades
Design Clare Barber and Kate Haynes
Illustrations Melvyn Evans
Photographer Andrew Perris

Printed in China

10 9 8 7 6 5 4 3 2

Important!
Safety warning: Felties are not toys.
Many have small, removable parts and should
be kept out of the reach of small children.

Contents

Starting Out

Hints and tips on making your first felt dolls

One of the things that makes felties so cute is their diminutive size—and this size is also almost the only challenge to making them successfully. Unless you're already used to working on such a small scale, start with a dark-colored doll, not a white one (when you're starting out, you'll be likely to handle the felt more, and the paler colors may become grubby as you work). Cut out the pieces accurately, and work slowly and meticulously—it's the crisp finish that lends the felties a lot of their charm. What's more, felt doesn't fray, so it's good for working at this tiny scale.

Tools

Use sharp scissors for cutting and snipping, and choose the smallest embroidery needle you're comfortable with to add details and sew the felties together.

The kind of craft glue that comes in a tube with a tiny nozzle dispenser is easiest to use;

alternatively, use a glue stick and, when glue is needed for a very tiny area, scrape a little off and use the point of a needle or a matchstick or toothpick to apply it accurately.

A disappearing marking pen is best for drawing around templates. These are popular with quilters and are available at most craft stores, and draw a fine line on fabric that simply disappears after a few days. You can also use it to mark stitching lines on the felt pieces.

Templates

Either trace the templates using tracing paper or—even easier—photocopy the template pages at 100 percent. Cut out the templates and draw around them onto the felt, then cut out your pattern pieces. When the pieces are particularly tiny, you may find it helps to scrape a very thin layer of glue over the wrong side of the felt and allow it to dry before you cut out the pieces: this makes the fabric slightly stiffer, and the cut pieces will have nice sharp edges.

Stuffing the Dolls

Use a customized toy stuffing for filling your felties: it is light, and it's also easy to separate out the minute wisps needed for stuffing the dolls. Don't use cotton balls or wadding, as they may clump and make for a lumpy little doll. We've suggested that you use a matchstick or toothpick to help you to distribute the stuffing evenly in the tinier pieces.

Sewing & Embroidery

All the felties are both embroidered and stitched together with embroidery floss. Standard floss comes in a small skein, with thread made up of six separate strands. You can pull apart strands to get the thickness specified in the patterns. You'll find that floss is used in single or double threads in most of the instructions, although three strands will occasionally be called for in specific patterns or stitches. To get the number of threads you want, cut a short length of floss 12–16 inches (30–40cm) long, and simply separate the desired number of strands from the main piece, pulling gently from one end. Keep the other strands to use elsewhere. To secure the thread, either tie a small knot at the end of the floss, or make a tiny cross stitch (one stitch laid over another).

Whichever method you choose, start from the wrong side of the felt piece on which you are working. All the patterns specify using an embroidery needle unless you are sewing on beads, in which case, you should use a special beading needle. This is a needle with a very narrow head so that the beads slip over it easily.

If you aren't used to embroidering, practice the stitches a few times on a felt scrap before working on a doll. None of the stitches described are difficult, but one or two—French knots in particular—can take some practice to get perfect.

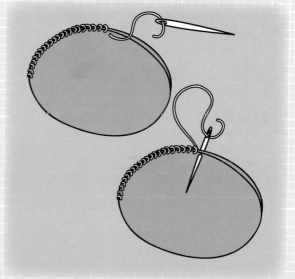

The Stitches

Overstitching

Overstitching is used to attach two pieces of fabric. This isn't a decorative stitch, so always use thread that matches the color of the felt, and make the stitches small and neat.

1 Take a strand of embroidery thread and align the two pieces to be stitched together. Bring the thread through from the wrong side of one piece and make a small stitch at right angles to the edges of the felt pieces, going over both edges and taking the needle through both layers of felt.

2 Push the needle back through the felt, bringing it out a little farther along from where you started, and make a second stitch over the edges of both pieces of felt.

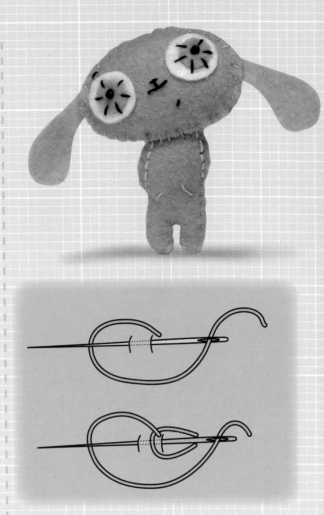

Backstitch

This stitch makes a plain unbroken line.

1 Thread the needle with one or two strands of floss, as directed, then bring it up through the fabric at the point at which you want the line of stitching to start.

2 Make a stitch going in the opposite direction to the way you want your backstitch line to continue, and bring the needle back up through the fabric one stitch length away in the direction in which you want your stitching line to go.

3 Take the thread backward and push the needle through the point where the first stitch finished. Bring it out one stitch length in front of the thread. Continue until the length of the desired line of backstitch is complete. Fasten off.

Chain Stitch

This stitch makes a decorative row of linked loops.

1 Bring your threaded needle up through the fabric, then bring the spare thread out in front of your needle, and make a loop around it. Reinsert the needle in the fabric and bring it out again one stitch length in front of your first stitch and through the loop of thread.

2 Pull the thread tightly enough to make an oval-shaped stitch that lies flat. Repeat both steps to continue the chain of stitches.

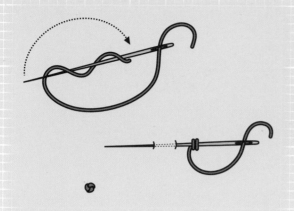

French Knot

This stitch makes a small decorative knot that stands above the surface of the felt.

1 Thread a needle with the number of strands specified in the instructions, fasten the end on the wrong side of the felt, and bring the needle out on the right side where you want to make your French knot. Use your left thumb to hold down the thread at the point at which it emerges from the felt, and wrap the thread twice around the needle.

2 Keep your thumb in place on the felt and bring the needle back to the starting point. Put its point back through the felt very close to where it emerged (not in the exact same spot, though, or the thread will simply pull back through the hole).

3 Push the needle through to the back of the felt and pull the thread taut. A small textured knot will be left on the right side of the felt. Fasten off the thread on the wrong side, or go on to make your next French knot.

Double and triple French knots are made by winding the thread two or three times more around the needle. This makes a larger finished knot, but you be very careful when pulling the thread back through so that it doesn't tangle.

Beading

Use a beading needle to add beads and sequins. Beads are sewn on simply by bringing the needle through from the back of the felt, threading the bead onto the needle, then pushing the needle back through near where it first emerged and pulling the thread tight.

To add a sequin, bring the needle up through the felt, thread on the sequin, and secure it by taking a stitch over to the edge on each side (or use more stitches, to make a decorative star shape on top of your sequin). Alternatively, use a bead to secure the sequin in the center, as shown below.

To Secure a Sequin with a Bead

1 Thread a beading needle and bring it up through the felt to the right side. Thread first the sequin, then the bead, onto the needle.

2 Take the needle back through the central hole of the sequin, pull the thread tight, and fasten off securely at the back of the felt. The bead, larger than the central hole of the sequin, will hold the sequin in place.

3 To add more beads, make a short stitch to the next point and add the bead. Repeat or fasten off securely at the back.

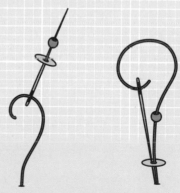

Babushka

Although this little Babushka is shown on her own, she's one of a traditional family of Russian nesting dolls. When you've made her, you can try scaling the pattern up or down on a photocopier to give her a family of sisters. Vary the decoration, too, if you like—but don't overdo it, or you will spoil her native folk-art air.

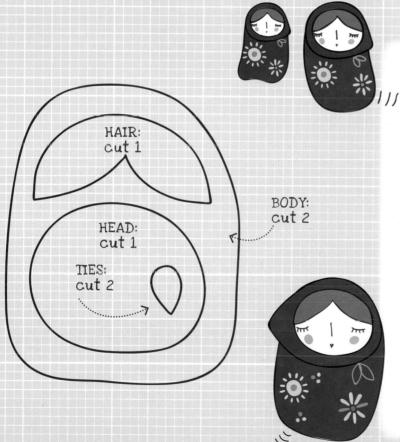

HAIR: cut 1

HEAD: cut 1

TIES: cut 2

BODY: cut 2

YOU WILL NEED

★ 6-inch (15-cm) square of fuchsia felt

★ Small scraps of brown and white felt

★ Embroidery floss in black, red, brown, white, and fuchsia

★ Packet of mixed beads and sequins

★ Tiny quantity of toy stuffing

★ Embroidery needle

★ Beading needle

★ Scissors

★ Red pencil

★ Tracing paper

★ Craft glue

★ Toothpick or matchstick

To make Babushka

1 Trace off the pattern pieces on page 9 onto tracing paper and cut out to make templates. Cut out 2 pieces each for the body and for the tiny headscarf ties from the fuchsia felt, 1 piece for the face from the white felt, and 1 for the hair from the brown felt.

2 Carefully position the hair at the top of the face piece, and attach in place with a small amount of craft glue.

3 Thread an embroidery needle with two strands of black embroidery floss and carefully hand-stitch the eyes and nose, using single straight stitches and checking against the photograph to get the positioning just right.

4 Now thread an embroidery needle with two strands of red embroidery floss and make Babushka's mouth. Hand-stitch tiny straight stitches horizontally and vertically, to make a rosebud-shaped mouth. Check the photograph to get the expression right.

5 Glue the head and hair into position on one of the body pieces, using a sparing amount of craft glue. Overstitch around the edges of the hair using an embroidery needle threaded with a single strand of brown embroidery floss. Use a needle threaded with a single strand of white embroidery floss to do the same around the edge of face. Fasten off the threads on the wrong side of the body piece.

6 Use a tiny dot of craft glue to attach the two little scarf ties in position. Thread an embroidery needle with two strands of fuchsia embroidery floss and backstitch a line across the body to give the headscarf an "edge," looking at the photograph to position it correctly.

7 Thread a beading needle with one strand of fuchsia embroidery floss and sew on the sequins and beads for decoration. Follow the arrangement shown in the photograph or make your own design, but remember if you do that little groups usually look better than single scattered beads. Attach the sequins with a central bead, using the instructions on page 7. Fasten the thread on the wrong side of the felt.

8 Align the second felt body piece with the first. Thread an embroidery needle with one strand of fuchsia embroidery floss and use a small overstitch to sew the pieces together. Leave a gap at the base of the doll (don't fasten off the thread) and fill her with a tiny amount of toy stuffing, using a toothpick or a matchstick to help you get the padding even. Don't use too much filling; she should be lightly padded, not stuffed. When the padding is distributed, stitch the gap closed.

9 Finally, give Babushka a light flush on the cheeks with a tiny touch of red pencil. Practice on a scrap of felt first to ensure that you give her just the right amount of color. She should have a rosy glow—not be blazing red.

Little Lion

There's nothing fierce about this tiny plains-dweller: in fact he looks slightly bewildered to find himself in more urban surroundings. As to whether he'd be more ready to roar or purr if you stroked him, our bet is on the latter. If you can crochet, make a little chain of yarn for his tail; if not, a tiny strip of felt does just as well.

YOU WILL NEED

- ★ 6-inch (15-cm) square of beige felt
- ★ 3-inch (7.5-cm) square of yellow felt
- ★ Small scrap of white felt
- ★ Embroidery floss in black, beige, and chocolate brown
- ★ 2 tiny black beads
- ★ Tiny quantity of beige yarn and crochet hook (if you want to crochet the tail)
- ★ Tiny quantity of toy stuffing
- ★ Embroidery needle
- ★ Beading needle
- ★ Scissors
- ★ Pencil
- ★ Tracing paper
- ★ Craft glue
- ★ Toothpick or matchstick

MANE: cut 1

NOSE: cut 1

BODY: cut 2

ARMS: cut 2

To make Little Lion

1 Trace off the pattern pieces on page 13 onto tracing paper and cut out to make templates. Cut out 2 pieces each for the body and for the arms from the beige felt (plus a narrow strip for the tail if you prefer not to crochet it), 1 piece for the mane from the yellow felt, and 1 piece for the nose patch from the white felt.

2 Thread an embroidery needle with 2 strands of black embroidery floss and embroider the nose onto the nose patch, using 2 straight horizontal stitches and 1 longer vertical one. Using the same thread, embroider a French knot under the nose to make the mouth. Knot the thread on the wrong side of the felt. Use a sparing amount of craft glue to fix the nose patch onto one of the felt body pieces, positioning it just below center in the middle of the face. Next, stitch the whiskers across the nose patch and the face, using 4 horizontal stitches. Check the photograph to help you position the parts correctly.

3 Still using 2 strands of black floss, stitch 2 tiny eyebrows, checking against the photograph to position them correctly. Next, thread a beading needle with 1 strand of black embroidery floss and stitch the 2 beads on for the eyes, placing them just under the eyebrows.

4 Now, again using the embroidery needle, threaded with 2 strands of black floss, add a belly button, low on the body, by embroidering a French knot.

5 Turn the embroidered body piece face down and glue the mane and arms in place on the wrong side, using a small quantity of craft glue.

6 Make the tail. Either crochet a little chain (the one in the photograph is 10 stitches long) or use a strip of beige felt cut from the template. For the crochet version, thread the yarn through the remaining body piece at the right point and fasten off on the wrong side. If you are using felt, simply glue the tail in place, or stitch it in place with a couple of strands of beige embroidery floss.

7 Give the tail a bushy tassel on its end by threading an embroidery needle with 2 strands of chocolate embroidery floss and passing it through the tip of the tail several times, leaving a small loop each time. Fasten off the thread into the tail so that it is not visible, and cut through the loops to make a little brush.

8 Align the 2 body pieces together, right sides out, and thread an embroidery needle with 1 strand of beige embroidery floss. Stitch the pieces together around the edges of the body using a neat overstitch, sewing through all 3 layers of felt in the mane area. Leave a gap along the base of the legs (don't fasten off the thread) and fill the lion with a tiny amount of toy stuffing, using a toothpick or a matchstick to help you to get the padding even. Don't use too much filling; he should be lightly padded. When the padding is evenly distributed, stitch the gap closed.

1

2

3

Glue the mane and arms in place

4

5

6

7

8

Panda

Is it the perpetual munching of bamboo that gives this miniature panda his spaced-out expression? Or is he simply a bit myopic? Whichever it is, he's still clasping a stalk of greenery firmly in his paw, and the wry twist to his mouth and surprised blush suggest that his snack has been interrupted for only a minute or two.

YOU WILL NEED

- ★ 6-inch (15-cm) square of white felt
- ★ 3-inch (7.5-cm) square of black felt
- ★ Small scraps of brown and green felt
- ★ Embroidery floss in black and white
- ★ Tiny quantity of toy stuffing
- ★ Embroidery needle
- ★ Scissors
- ★ Pencil
- ★ Red pencil
- ★ Tracing paper
- ★ Craft glue
- ★ Toothpick or matchstick

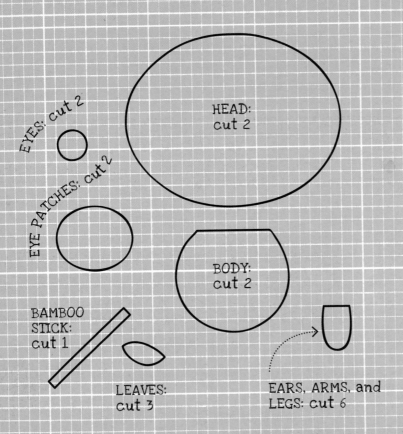

EYES: cut 2

EYE PATCHES: cut 2

HEAD: cut 2

BODY: cut 2

BAMBOO STICK: cut 1

LEAVES: cut 3

EARS, ARMS, and LEGS: cut 6

To make Panda

1 Trace off the pattern pieces on page 16 onto tracing paper and cut out to make templates. Cut out 2 pieces each for the body, head, and eyes from the white felt; 2 pieces for the eye patches and 2 identical pieces for the arms, legs, and ears from the black felt; 1 piece for the bamboo stem from the brown felt, and 3 little leaves from the green. Take 1 of the head pieces and use a little craft glue to stick the black eye patches in position, checking against the photograph or illustration to position them correctly. Stick a white eye near the top of each eye patch.

2 Thread an embroidery needle with 2 strands of black floss and embroider the nose, mouth, and brows on the face. The nose is made with 2 tiny stitches, 1 horizontal and 1 vertical, making a "T" shape; the brows are 1 small, angled straight stitch each, and the mouth is another single stitch, but placed off-center and at a slight angle to give Panda his quizzical expression.

3 Take 2 of the identical black felt pieces, and a little craft glue to stick Panda's ears on the wrong side of the embroidered face. Thread an embroidery needle with 1 strand of white embroidery floss, align the head pieces with one another, and sew together using a small neat overstitch. Leave a gap at the bottom of the head (don't fasten off the thread) and fill it with a tiny amount of toy stuffing, using a toothpick or a matchstick to get the padding even. Don't overfill; it should be lightly padded, not stuffed. When the padding is evenly distributed, stitch the gap shut.

4 Use a small amount of craft glue to stick the remaining 4 identical black felt pieces onto the back of one of the body pieces for the arms and legs, referring to the photograph to position them correctly.

5 Make a belly button by sewing a French knot low on the second body piece, using 2 strands of black embroidery floss and an embroidery needle.

6 Align the 2 body pieces together, right sides out. Thread an embroidery needle with 1 strand of white embroidery floss and use a small overstitch to sew the body pieces together. Leave the top open, fill with a small quantity of toy stuffing, distributing it evenly, then sew shut. Position the head so it overlaps the body and, using 1 strand of white embroidery floss, sew the body and head together, stitching through all 4 layers of felt. Place the new stitches over the earlier overstitching for a neat finish.

7 Use a little craft glue to stick the leaves onto the stem of bamboo, then glue the bamboo in place on Panda's body, so it looks as though he is holding it in his paw.

8 Finally, use the red pencil to add a touch of color to Panda's cheeks.

1

2

3

4

5

6

Keep the color on the panda's cheeks subtle

7

8

MuShroom Girl

Lightly dozing, Mushroom Girl is lost in a forest reverie. Her cheerful red-and-white spotted hat tops off her stalk of a body and her pale pink face; in fact, her coloring is really closer to that of a toadstool. Whichever family she belongs to, though, her sweet, downcast look and cute flower embroidery are pure feltie.

YOU WILL NEED

- ★ 3-inch (7.5-cm) square of red-and-white polka-dot felt (you can find this online or in craft stores)
- ★ Small scraps of pale cream, white, and green felt
- ★ Embroidery floss in red, pink, green, and white
- ★ 12 tiny red beads
- ★ 2 tiny pink beads
- ★ 1 red and 1 pink sequin
- ★ Tiny quantity of toy stuffing
- ★ Embroidery needle
- ★ Beading needle
- ★ Scissors
- ★ Pencil
- ★ Tracing paper
- ★ Craft glue
- ★ Toothpick or matchstick

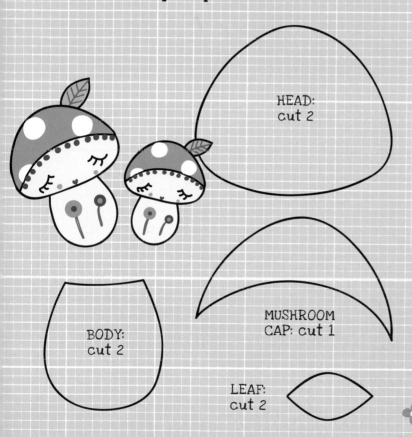

HEAD: cut 2

BODY: cut 2

MUSHROOM CAP: cut 1

LEAF: cut 2

To make Mushroom Girl

1 Trace off the pattern pieces on page 21 onto tracing paper and cut out to make templates. Cut 1 cap piece from the red-and-white felt, 2 head pieces, 1 from the pale cream felt and 1 from the red-and-white felt, 2 body pieces from the white felt, and 2 tiny leaves from the green felt. Thread an embroidery needle with 2 strands of black embroidery floss and sew the eyes and lashes onto the cream face piece, checking against the photograph to get the placement right. The eyes are made using 3 curving backstitches, and the eyelashes with 4 small straight stitches for each eye.

2 Thread an embroidery needle with 2 strands of red floss and make the mouth with a little French knot. Rethread the needle with 2 strands of pink floss and embroider the cheeks with tiny circles of chain stitch.

3 Stick the red-and-white cap onto the head with a little craft glue. Thread a beading needle with 1 strand of red floss. Sew the 12 tiny red beads along the edge of the cap. Fasten off the thread on the wrong side facing out.

4 Thread an embroidery needle with 2 strands of green floss; embroider the veins on 1 of the felt leaves, using small straight stitches. Fasten off the thread on the wrong side, then use a dab of craft glue to stick the leaves together. Glue the leaf onto the wrong side of the red-and-white cap.

5 Align the 2 head pieces together, right sides out. Thread an embroidery needle with 1 strand of red embroidery floss and overstitch along the top part of the head, sewing through all 3 layers of felt. Rethread the needle with 1 strand of white floss and overstitch the edge of the cream face closed at each end, stopping in the middle to lightly pad the head with a little stuffing before closing the gap completely.

6 Thread an embroidery needle with 2 strands of green floss and embroider 2 stems and 4 leaves onto 1 of the body pieces. The stems are made from 4 chain stitches; each leaf is made from a single chain stitch. Thread a beading needle with 1 strand of pink floss and add a sequin secured by a bead (as shown on page 7), to make a flower at the top of each stem. Fasten off on the wrong side.

7 Align the 2 body pieces together, right side of embroidery facing out. Thread an embroidery needle with 1 strand of white embroidery floss and overstitch the pieces together using small stitches, leaving the top open. Pad with a small quantity of toy stuffing, using a matchstick or a toothpick to distribute it evenly, then sew shut.

8 Position the head so that it overlaps the body. Using 1 strand of white embroidery floss and overstitch the body and head together, stitching through all 4 layers of felt. Place the new stitches over the earlier overstitching for a neat finish.

Sun-Loving Rat

With an ice-cream cone in one paw and sunglasses large enough to satisfy the most ardent fashionista, this cheery rat is clearly an enthusiast of sunny climates. All she needs are a lounger, a towel, and plenty of sunscreen for her sensitive ears and tail, and she'll be ready to soak up the rays.

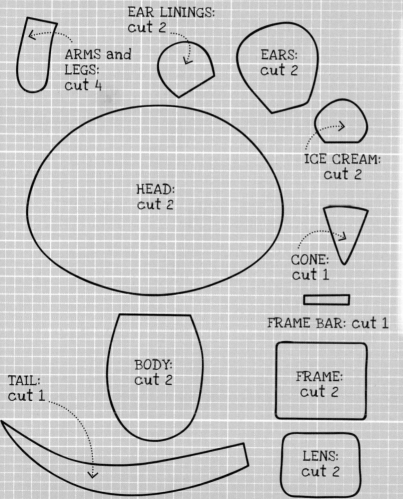

EAR LININGS:
cut 2

ARMS and LEGS:
cut 4

EARS:
cut 2

ICE CREAM:
cut 2

HEAD:
cut 2

CONE:
cut 1

FRAME BAR: cut 1

TAIL:
cut 1

BODY:
cut 2

FRAME:
cut 2

LENS:
cut 2

YOU WILL NEED

- ★ 6-inch (15-cm) square of gray felt
- ★ Small scraps of pink, white, black, green, and cream felt
- ★ Embroidery floss in white, black, gray, chocolate brown, and green
- ★ Tiny quantity of toy stuffing
- ★ Embroidery needle
- ★ Scissors
- ★ Pencil
- ★ Tracing paper
- ★ Craft glue
- ★ Toothpick or matchstick

To make Sun-Loving Rat

1 Trace off the pattern pieces on page 25 onto tracing paper and cut out to make templates. This feltie has a lot of separate pieces: cut 2 head pieces, 2 body pieces, and 2 ears from the gray felt; 4 pieces for the arms and legs, 2 ear linings, and 1 tail from the pink felt; 2 sunglass frames and 1 frame bar from the white felt; and 2 lens pieces from the black felt. Finally, cut 2 pieces from the green felt for the scoop of ice cream, and 1 piece from the cream felt for the cone.

2 Use a little craft glue to stick the lenses into the centers of the sunglass frames. Glue the frame bar across the center of one of the face pieces, then stick on a frame at either end of it. Thread an embroidery needle with 1 strand of white embroidery floss and sew around the sunglass frames with a small, neat overstitch. Rethread the needle with 2 strands of black floss and stitch 2 whiskers onto each side of the face, each with a single long straight stitch. Make a tiny nose with 3 small straight stitches arranged in a triangle, and a crooked mouth with 2 straight stitches in an inverted "V" shape, the left-hand one longer than the right. Finally, thread an embroidery needle with 2 strands of white floss and fill in the nose with a tiny French knot.

3 Use a little craft glue to stick the pink ear linings into the ears. Glue the ears in position on one side of the second head piece. Align the two head pieces together, right sides out. Thread an embroidery needle with 1 strand of gray floss and sew the pieces together with a small overstitch. Leave a gap at the base of the head (don't fasten off the thread), and fill it with a tiny amount of toy stuffing, using a toothpick or a matchstick to get the padding even. When the padding is distributed, overstitch the gap closed.

4 Stick the arms and legs in position on the wrong side of one body piece, using craft glue. Carefully make a tiny slit with scissors near the bottom of the back. Gently push the blunt end of the tail piece through the slit; use a dab of craft glue at the base of the tail to hold in place.

5 Thread an embroidery needle with 2 strands of black embroidery floss. Stitch a French knot near the bottom of the second body piece for the belly button. Fasten off on the wrong side. Align the body pieces together, right sides out. Thread an embroidery needle with 1 strand of gray floss and use a small overstitch to sew them together around the edge. Leave a gap at the top of the body (don't fasten off the thread), and fill it with a tiny amount of toy stuffing. When the body is padded, stitch the gap shut.

6 Position the head so that it overlaps the body. Thread a needle with 1 strand of gray floss and use a small overstitch to fix the head and body together, stitching through all layers of felt. Try to place the new stitches over the earlier ones.

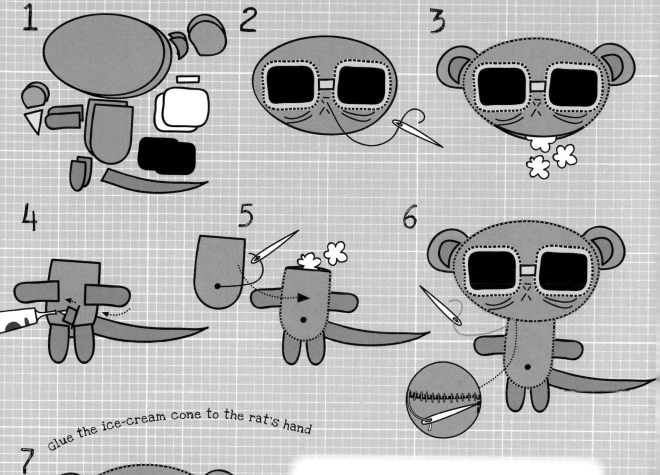

1

2

3

4

5

6

Glue the ice-cream cone to the rat's hand

7 Finally, make the ice-cream cone. Thread an embroidery needle with 2 strands of chocolate brown floss and sew a few tiny French knots on one piece of green felt to add the chocolate chips. Align the two pieces of green felt together, with the embroidery facing right side out, and join them with a tiny overstitch using 1 strand of green floss. Fasten off the thread, and glue the ice cream to the cone. Attach the cone to the rat's hand with a dab of craft glue.

Polar-roo

A feltie polar bear with marsupial tendencies—her cub is carried in a neat pouch—this little creature is easy to make. The pure white needs to stay that way, though, so make sure that you always work with clean hands and, when it comes to adding a tiny blush to the cheeks, wield your pencil with care—you want only a mere suggestion of delicate color.

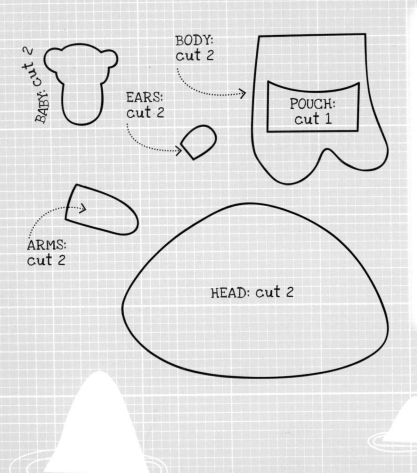

BABY: cut 2

EARS: cut 2

BODY: cut 2

POUCH: cut 1

ARMS: cut 2

HEAD: cut 2

YOU WILL NEED

- ★ 6-inch (15-cm) square of white felt
- ★ Embroidery floss in black and white
- ★ Tiny quantity of toy stuffing
- ★ Embroidery needle
- ★ Scissors
- ★ Pencil
- ★ Black pencil
- ★ Red pencil
- ★ Tracing paper
- ★ Craft glue
- ★ Toothpick or matchstick

To make Polar-roo

1 Trace off the pattern pieces on page 28 onto tracing paper and cut out to make templates. Use to cut out the pattern pieces, all from white felt: 2 pieces each for the head, body, arms, ears, tiny baby bear, and 1 for his pouch. Thread an embroidery needle with 3 strands of black embroidery floss and sew the eyes and nose onto the head piece, checking against the photograph to position them correctly. Make the eyes with a large French knot, surrounded by 3 single straight stitches to make Polar-roo's eyelashes. The nose is 3 horizontal straight stitches in an inverted triangle shape, with 2 tiny stitches in an inverted "V" shape just below them. Fasten off the thread on the wrong side of the felt. Use craft glue to stick the ears in position on the wrong side of the second head piece.

2 Align both head pieces together, right sides out. Thread an embroidery needle with 1 strand of white embroidery floss and use a tiny overstitch to sew the pieces together. Leave a gap at the base of the head (don't fasten off the thread) and fill it evenly with a tiny amount of toy stuffing. Stitch the gap closed.

3 Glue the arms onto the back of one of the body pieces. Turn the piece right side up. Position the pouch on the front of the body and sew it on, using 1 strand of white floss to overstitch the pouch in place, leaving the top of the pouch open to make a pocket. Allow a little fullness as you stitch, to make it easier to fit the baby into it.

4 Align the 2 body pieces, right sides out. Sew together with a small overstitch using 1 strand of white floss. Leave a gap at the top of the body and pad it lightly and evenly with tiny wisps of toy stuffing. Overstitch the gap closed.

5 Position the head pieces so that they overlap the body. Using 1 strand of white floss and a small overstitch, sew the head and body together, stitching through all layers of felt. Place the new stitches over the earlier ones to keep the end result neat.

6 Sew the features on Baby Roo's face. Thread an embroidery needle with 2 strands of black floss and make 2 small French knots for the eyes. The mouth is made with 2 tiny straight stitches in a cross shape. Fasten off the thread on the wrong side of the felt.

7 Align the 2 pieces of the baby's body, then sew together using 1 strand of white floss and a small overstitch. Partway through, pad his body with a minute amount of stuffing (you may need to use the blunt end of a needle to help you distribute it evenly), then stitch him closed and pop him into his pouch.

8 Make Polar-roo's darker inner ears and claws with small strokes of a black pencil, and add a faint blush to her cheeks with a red pencil. Practice on a scrap of white felt before you tackle the final doll.

1

2

3

4

5

6

7

8

Be sparing when adding cheek color

Pensive Rabbit

Eyes raised skyward—perhaps he's stargazing?—and hands clasped behind him, this small rabbit seems a little fey and thoughtful. A pastel blue and turquoise color scheme matches his wistful looks, while wide green eyes emphasize his slightly other worldly quality. All in all, he makes a perfect companion for your bedside table: he can watch over you while you sleep.

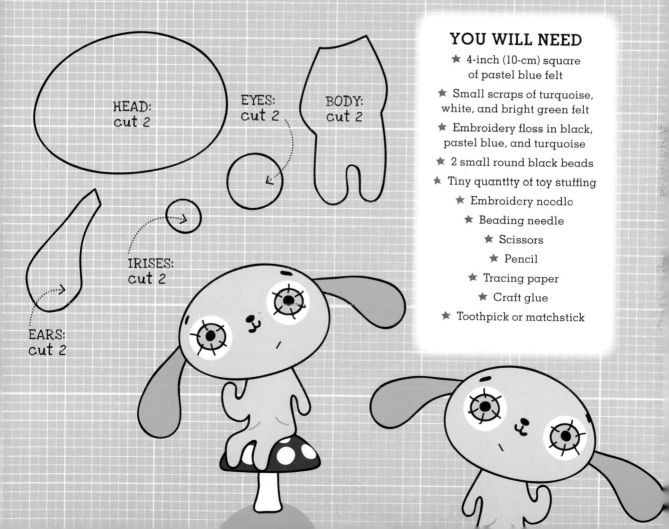

HEAD: cut 2

EYES: cut 2

BODY: cut 2

IRISES: cut 2

EARS: cut 2

YOU WILL NEED

★ 4-inch (10-cm) square of pastel blue felt

★ Small scraps of turquoise, white, and bright green felt

★ Embroidery floss in black, pastel blue, and turquoise

★ 2 small round black beads

★ Tiny quantity of toy stuffing

★ Embroidery needle

★ Beading needle

★ Scissors

★ Pencil

★ Tracing paper

★ Craft glue

★ Toothpick or matchstick

To make Pensive Rabbit

1 Trace off the pattern pieces on page 33 onto tracing paper and cut out to make templates. Cut out 2 pieces each for the body and the head from the pastel blue felt, 2 ears from the turquoise felt, 2 eyes from the white felt, and 2 irises from the bright green felt. Using tiny dots of craft glue, first glue the irises in the center of the eye pieces, then glue the eyes in position on one of the face pieces, checking against the photograph to position them correctly.

2 Thread a beading needle with 2 strands of black embroidery floss and carefully stitch a black bead in the center of each eye. Sew 6 short, straight stitches around the edge of each iris to give Pensive Rabbit his characteristic eyes-wide-open expression.

3 Now thread an embroidery needle with 2 strands of black embroidery floss and make Rabbit's eyebrows by sewing 2 tiny straight stitches for each one and placing at a slight angle. Stitch his nose and mouth using 3 stitches— a short horizontal, a short vertical, and a longer horizontal—arranged as shown in the photograph. Finally make his mouth, which is a single off-center short stitch.

4 Use craft glue to fix the ears in position on the wrong side of the second head piece.

5 Align the 2 head pieces together, right sides out. Thread an embroidery needle with a single strand of pastel blue embroidery floss and sew the 2 head pieces together with a small, neat overstitch. Leave a gap at the base of the head (don't fasten off the thread) and fill it with a tiny amount of toy stuffing, using a toothpick or matchstick to help to distribute it evenly. Overstitch the gap closed.

6 Thread an embroidery needle with 2 strands of turquoise embroidery floss and outline Pensive Rabbit's arms with 2 lines of backstitch along the sides of his body. Check against the photograph to help you position them. Embroider his pockets with two single straight stitches at a slight angle as shown.

7 Thread an embroidery needle with 1 strand of pastel blue floss, align the 2 body pieces, and sew them together using a small overstitch. Leave a gap at the neck (don't fasten off the thread) and fill Pensive Rabbit's body with a tiny amount of toy stuffing, using a toothpick or a matchstick to help to distribute it evenly. Don't use too much filling; he should be lightly padded, not stuffed. Stitch the gap closed.

8 Place Pensive Rabbit's head so that it overlaps his body at a slight angle. Using an embroidery needle and 1 strand of pastel blue embroidery floss, attach the head to the body using a small, neat overstitch, stitching through all 4 layers of felt. Try to place the new stitches over the earlier ones to give a neat finish.

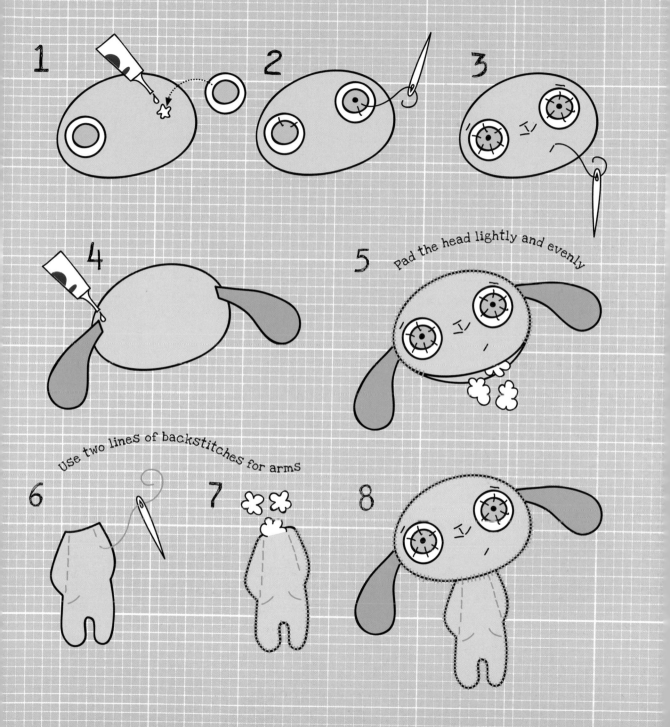

1

2

3

4

5 Pad the head lightly and evenly

Use two lines of backstitches for arms

6

7

8

Sleepy Fox

Not even the prospect of a juicy chicken could awaken this dozy little fox cub, sweetly asleep in a patch of sun. Even for a feltie, he's tiny, measuring a scant two and half inches from pricked ear to tail tip. Make sure that you use the tiniest wisps of toy stuffing to pad him, and take care to sew your tiniest stitches when you're putting him together.

YOU WILL NEED

- ★ 4-inch (10-cm) square of brown felt
- ★ Small scraps of beige and black felt
- ★ Embroidery floss in black and chocolate brown
- ★ Tiny quantity of toy stuffing
- ★ Embroidery needle
- ★ Scissors
- ★ Pencil
- ★ Fine black felt-tip pen
- ★ Tracing paper
- ★ Craft glue
- ★ Toothpick or matchstick

BODY:
cut 2

TAIL:
cut 2

LEGS:
cut 2

LEFT ARM:
cut 1

EYE PATCH:
cut 1

TAILTIP:
cut 1

RIGHT ARM:
cut 1

HEAD:
cut 2

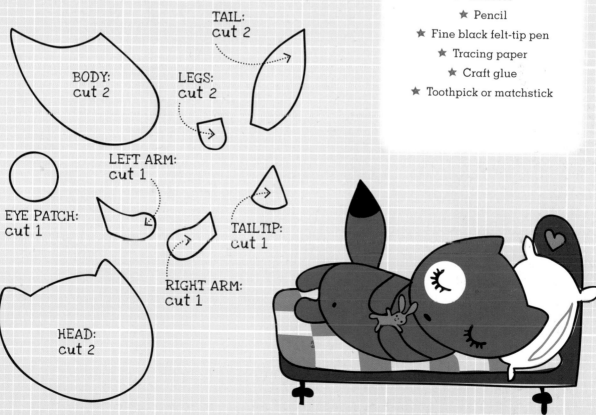

To make Sleepy Fox

1 Trace off the pattern pieces on page 37 onto tracing paper and cut out to make templates. Cut out 2 pieces each for the body, head, tail, and 2 separate legs and arms from the brown felt; 1 small circle for the eye patch from the beige felt; and 1 tail tip from the black felt. Using a little craft glue, stick the eye patch in position on the left side of one of the head pieces.

2 Thread an embroidery needle with 2 strands of black embroidery floss and sew 2 small semicircles in backstitch to make the eyes, one quite low on the eye patch and the other on the right-hand side of the face. Each eye is made using four stitches. Make 1 tiny straight stitch for Sleepy Fox's mouth.

3 Thread an embroidery needle with 1 strand of chocolate brown embroidery floss. Align the 2 head pieces, right sides facing out, and stitch together using a small, neat overstitch. Leave a gap at the base of the head (don't fasten off the thread) and fill it with a tiny amount of toy stuffing, using a toothpick or matchstick to arrange it evenly. Overstitch the gap closed.

4 Use small dots of craft glue to stick the legs onto the wrong side of one of the body pieces. Check against the photograph before you glue them in place to get the position right.

5 Turn the body piece right side up and stick on the arms with a little craft glue. Thread an embroidery needle with 2 strands of black embroidery floss and make the belly button with a tiny cross stitch, positioned low on the stomach.

6 Stick the black tail tip onto the right sides of one of the tail pieces, lining up the edges carefully and using just a tiny quantity of craft glue. Align the 2 tail pieces, right side out. Sew together with a small overstitch, using 1 strand of brown embroidery floss. Leave the base of the tail open (don't fasten the thread) and pad the tail lightly with a tiny quantity of toy stuffing. Go over the brown stitches on the black tip of the tail with black felt-tip pen.

7 Align the 2 body pieces, right sides out. Insert the tail in position between the two pieces, black tip facing toward the front. Thread an embroidery needle with 1 strand of chocolate brown embroidery floss. Sew the body together using a small overstitch, stitching through all 4 layers of felt where the tail is inserted and leaving the neck open. Lightly stuff the body with toy stuffing using a matchstick or toothpick to distribute evenly. Overstitch the gap closed.

8 Place Sleepy Fox's head so that it slightly overlaps his body, referring to the photograph to get the angle right. Using one strand of brown embroidery floss, sew the body and head together, stitching through all 4 layers of felt. Try to place the new stitches over the earlier overstitching to give a neat finish.

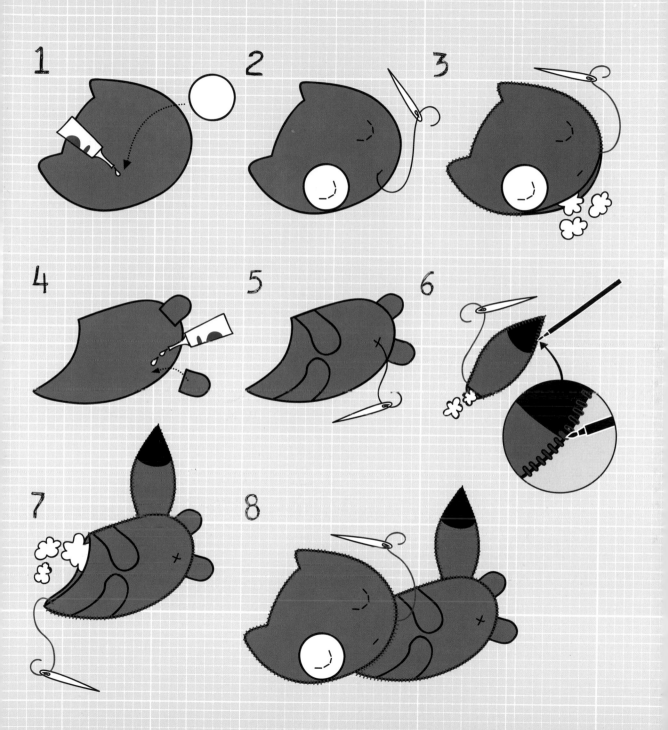

Sailor Puppy

With a smart Parisian-style color scheme of red and navy, this Sailor Puppy is all ready for her first voyage. Her minute striped sweater and jaunty beret look thoroughly seaworthy; all she needs is an appropriately stylish boat, and she can set sail right away...

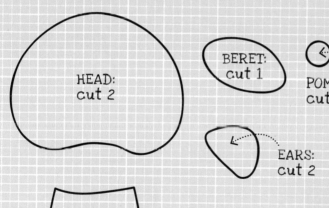

HEAD:
cut 2

BERET:
cut 1

POMPOM:
cut 1

EARS:
cut 2

BODY:
cut 2

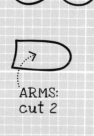

ARMS:
cut 2

YOU WILL NEED

★ 4-inch (10-cm) square of white felt

★ Small scraps of brown, blue, and red felt

★ Embroidery floss in black, white, and navy blue

★ 2 black bugle beads

★ 6-inch (15-cm) length of narrow navy blue ribbon

★ Tiny quantity of toy stuffing

★ Embroidery needle

★ Beading needle

★ Scissors

★ Pencil

★ Fine blue felt-tip pen

★ Tracing paper

★ Craft glue

★ Toothpick or matchstick

To make Sailor Puppy

1 Trace off the pattern pieces on page 41 onto tracing paper and cut out to make templates. Cut 2 pieces each for the body, head, and arms from the white felt; 2 pieces for the ears from the brown felt; 1 piece for the beret from the blue felt; and 1 piece for the pompom from the red felt. Thread a beading needle with 1 strand of black embroidery floss and sew the bugle beads vertically onto one of the head pieces, checking against the photograph to get the position right.

2 Thread an embroidery needle with 2 strands of black embroidery floss. Embroider the nose using 3 straight, overlapping horizontal stitches with a single vertical long straight stitch underneath them to make a "T" shape.

3 Thread an embroidery needle with 1 strand of white floss. Align the head pieces with each other and sew together, right sides out, using a small neat overstitch. Leave a gap at the base of the head (don't fasten off the thread) and fill it with a tiny amount of toy stuffing, using a toothpick or a matchstick to get the padding even. Don't use too much filling; it should be lightly padded, not stuffed. When the padding is evenly arranged, overstitch the gap closed.

4 Use a small amount of craft glue to stick the pompom onto the beret, then stick the beret and Sailor Puppy's ears onto her head.

5 Take 1 of the body pieces, and use a little craft glue to stick the arms in position on the wrong side.

6 Take the other body piece, and cut the navy ribbon into 3 pieces. Make them just slightly longer than the width of the body. Thread an embroidery needle with 1 strand of navy blue embroidery floss and stitch the ribbon in 3 evenly spaced stripes across the body using small, straight stitches. Fold the ends of the ribbon over to the inside (wrong side) of the body, and tack in place with a few stitches.

7 Align the 2 body pieces, right sides out. Use a needle threaded with 1 strand of white embroidery floss to overstitch the pieces together, leaving the neck open. Fill the puppy with a tiny amount of toy stuffing, using a toothpick or matchstick to get the padding even. When it is neatly arranged, overstitch the gap closed.

8 Position the head on top of the body, and overstitch the body and head together, stitching through all 4 layers of felt. Try to place the new stitches over the earlier overstitching for a neat finish. Finally, take a fine blue felt-tip pen and lightly color in any white stitches that lie over the navy blue ribbon where Sailor Puppy's body was sewn together.

1

2

3

4

5

6

7

8

Messenger Bear

The magazines and newspapers in Messenger Bear's bag are too tiny to read, but he's clearly an experienced courier. His professionally designed bag is worn efficiently around his neck, leaving his hands free to throw papers and periodicals onto his customers' front porches or to place them carefully into their mailboxes.

YOU WILL NEED

- ★ 6-inch (15-cm) square of light brown felt
- ★ Small scraps of turquoise, purple, and white felt
- ★ Embroidery floss in black, brown, and purple
- ★ 2 tiny black beads
- ★ Tiny quantity of toy stuffing
- ★ Tiny scrap of folded newsprint to fill the bag
- ★ Tiny sticker or sequin to "brand" the bag (optional)
- ★ Embroidery needle
- ★ Beading needle
- ★ Scissors
- ★ Pencil
- ★ Tracing paper
- ★ Craft glue
- ★ Toothpick or matchstick

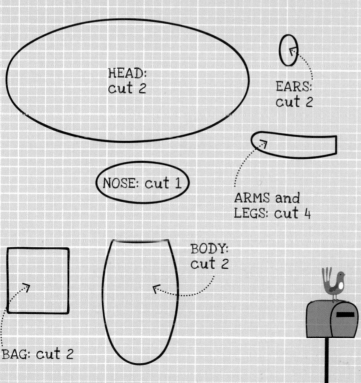

HEAD: cut 2

EARS: cut 2

NOSE: cut 1

ARMS and LEGS: cut 4

BODY: cut 2

BAG: cut 2

To make Messenger Bear

1 Trace off the pattern pieces on page 45 onto tracing paper and cut out to make templates. Cut out 2 head and 2 body pieces from the brown felt; 2 arms, 2 legs, and 2 ears from the turquoise felt; 2 bag pieces from the purple felt; and 1 nose piece from the white felt. Thread an embroidery needle with two strands of black embroidery floss and sew the nose and mouth onto the white nose patch. Make the nose with 2 tiny horizontal overlapping straight stitches, and a single vertical stitch. Add two curved horizontal stitches at the base of the vertical stitch for the mouth, following the positioning in the photograph. Glue the nose patch in position on one of the head pieces.

2 Thread a beading needle with 1 strand of black embroidery floss and sew the beads on to make the bear's eyes. Using an embroidery needle and 2 strands of black floss, add a few eyelashes, with short straight stitches.

3 Use craft glue to stick the ears in position on the wrong side of the second head piece.

4 Align the 2 head pieces together, right sides out. Thread an embroidery needle with 1 strand of brown embroidery floss, and sew them together with a small, neat overstitch. Leave a small gap open along the lower edge of the head (don't fasten off the thread), and fill it with toy stuffing, using a toothpick or a matchstick to get the padding even. When the padding is evenly distributed, overstitch the gap closed.

5 Use a little craft glue to stick the arms and legs on the wrong side of 1 body piece. Align with the second body piece, right sides out, and use 1 strand of brown embroidery floss to overstitch the body together. Leave an opening at the neck and lightly pad the body with toy stuffing, using a toothpick or matchstick to help you. When the padding is evenly distributed, overstitch the gap closed.

6 Thread an embroidery needle with 1 strand of brown embroidery floss. Position the head on the body and overstitch the body and head together, stitching through all 4 layers of felt. Try to place the new stitches over the earlier overstitching for a neat finish.

7 Align the 2 bag pieces together. Thread an embroidery needle with 2 strands of purple embroidery floss and overstitch the sides and bottom to make a pouch, leaving the top edge open. Leave a long tail of thread at the top right corner of the bag, pass it around Messenger Bear's neck to make the strap, then finish it off at the left-hand top corner of the bag, sewing the thread in and knotting the end securely.

8 Neatly fold a tiny scrap of newspaper and place it in the bag. You can also use a little dot of craft glue to add a sequin or a minute sticker to the front of the bag to "brand" it.

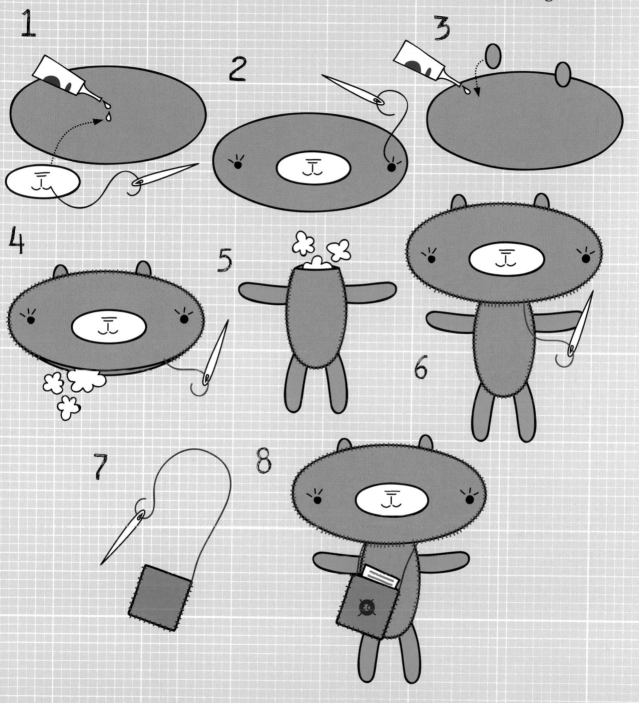

Cute Chihuahua

Even by toy breed standards, this Chihuahua is a miniature. But her upright ears and cheerily wagging tail tell you that she has got plenty of character. And luckily she has got a juicy bone, too—specially made to match her in scale.

NOSE:
cut 1

HEAD:
cut 2

TAIL:
cut 1

BODY:
cut 2

BONE:
cut 2

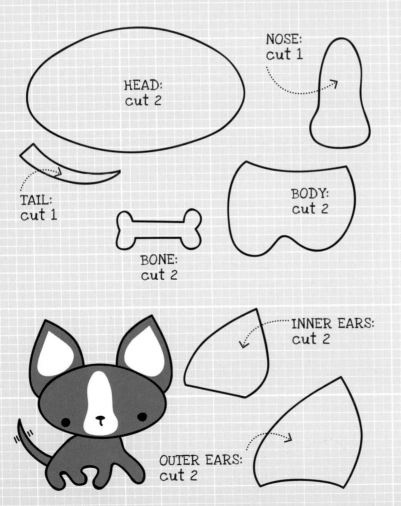

INNER EARS:
cut 2

OUTER EARS:
cut 2

YOU WILL NEED

- ★ 6-inch (15-cm) square of light brown felt
- ★ Small scrap of white felt
- ★ Embroidery floss in black and light brown
- ★ 2 round black or dark blue beads, ⅛ inch (3 cm) in diameter
- ★ Tiny quantity of toy stuffing
- ★ Embroidery needle
- ★ Beading needle
- ★ Scissors
- ★ Pencil
- ★ Disappearing marking pen
- ★ Tracing paper
- ★ Craft glue
- ★ Toothpick or matchstick

To make Cute Chihuahua

1 Trace off the pattern pieces on page 48 onto tracing paper and cut them out to make templates. Cut 2 head pieces, 2 body pieces, 2 outer ears, and 1 tail from the light brown felt; and 2 inner ear pieces, 2 bone pieces, and 1 nose patch from the white felt. Use the disappearing marking pen to outline the place where the nose patch will be on one of the head pieces. This will help you position the eyes and the ears correctly.

2 Thread a beading needle with 1 strand of black embroidery floss and stitch the beads in place to make the eyes.

3 Use a little craft glue to stick the inner ear pieces onto the outer ears. Next, position the ears on one side of the unused head piece, and use a little craft glue to stick them in place.

4 Align the two head pieces together, with the face right side up and the ears facing forward. Thread an embroidery needle with 1 strand of light brown embroidery floss, and sew the head together using a small, neat overstitch. Leave a small gap open along the lower edge (don't fasten off the thread) and fill the head with a tiny amount of toy stuffing, using a toothpick or a matchstick to get the padding even. When the padding is evenly distributed, stitch the gap closed.

5 Thread an embroidery needle with 2 strands of black embroidery floss and stitch the nose onto the nose piece, using 2 small straight stitches in a "T" shape.

6 Use a little craft glue to stick the tail in place on the wrong side of a body piece. Align the body pieces. Stitch together using 1 strand of light brown embroidery floss and a small, neat overstitch, and leave an opening at the neck. Lightly pad the body with a little toy stuffing, using a toothpick or matchstick to help you to get the padding even. When the padding is evenly distributed, stitch the body closed.

7 Position the head so that it overlaps the body, and use an embroidery needle and 1 strand of light brown embroidery floss to overstitch body and head together, stitching through all 4 layers of felt. Try to place the new stitches over the earlier ones for a neat finish.

8 Finally, glue the nose in position on the face where you marked earlier with the disappearing pen, and make the bone by gluing the two pieces together with a little craft glue.

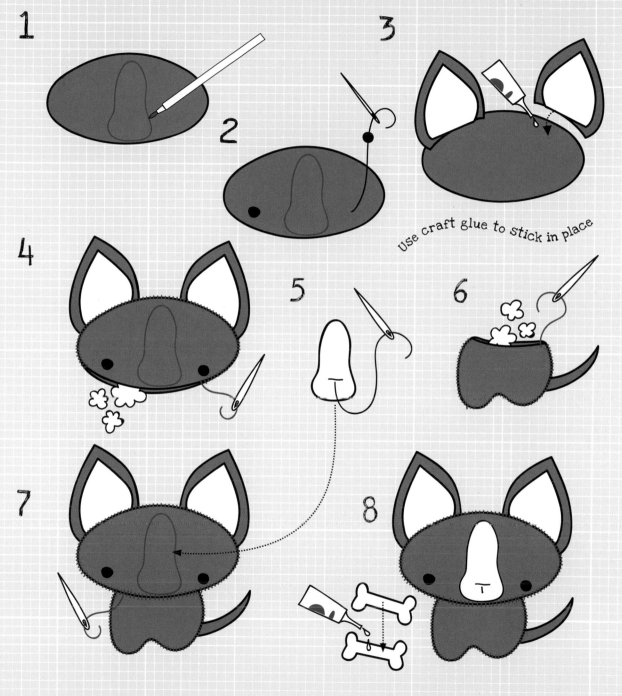

1

2

3

Use craft glue to stick in place

4

5

6

7

8

Curly Ram

Stepping straight out of some feltie version of the zodiac, this Aries ram has the full-blown horns that declare his "ram" status, but none of the accompanying aggression. Lamblike, he even wears a bell around his neck, so that you can keep track of his movements around your desktop or dressing table.

YOU WILL NEED

- ★ 6-inch (15-cm) square of chocolate brown felt
- ★ 4-inch (10-cm) square of orange felt
- ★ Small scrap of white felt
- ★ Embroidery floss in black, chocolate brown, and orange
- ★ 2 tiny black beads
- ★ 1 small bell (optional)
- ★ Tiny quantity of toy stuffing
- ★ Embroidery needle
- ★ Beading needle
- ★ Scissors
- ★ Pencil
- ★ Tracing paper
- ★ Craft glue
- ★ Toothpick or matchstick

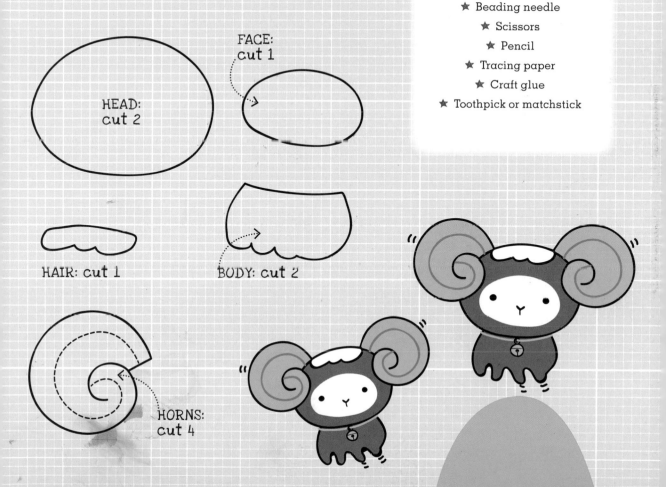

HEAD: cut 2

FACE: cut 1

HAIR: cut 1

BODY: cut 2

HORNS: cut 4

To make Curly Ram

1 Trace off the pattern pieces on page 53 onto tracing paper and cut out to make templates. Use to cut out the felt as follows: 2 pieces each for the head and body from the chocolate brown felt; 4 pieces for the horns from the orange felt; and 1 piece each for the face and woolly hair from the white felt. Thread a beading needle with 1 strand of black embroidery floss and sew the black beads for the eyes in position on the face. Now use an embroidery needle and 2 strands of black embroidery floss to embroider a "Y" shape, formed by 3 straight stitches, for the nose.

2 Use a little craft glue to stick the face in position on one of the head pieces.

3 Following the stitching line indicated on the pattern pieces, and using an embroidery needle threaded with 2 strands of chocolate brown embroidery floss, carefully backstitch a spiral down the centerline of 2 of the horn pieces. The stitching needs to appear on the front of each horn, so stitch 1 piece for the left-hand horn and 1 piece for the right-hand horn.

4 Now align each horn with its corresponding back piece. Using an embroidery needle threaded with 1 strand of orange embroidery floss, carefully sew together with a small, neat overstitch. You need to pad the horns as you sew because of the spiral shape; this is slightly fiddly but use tiny wisps of stuffing and a toothpick or matchstick to help you to get the padding even.

5 Align the two pieces for the head, and insert the wide ends of the horns in position between the pieces. Thread an embroidery needle with one strand of chocolate brown floss and sew the head together, sewing through all 4 layers of felt when you stitch in the horns. Leave the thinner spiral end of each horn free; it should curl freely in front of the face. Leave an opening at the lower edge of the head and pad with stuffing before stitching it closed.

6 Align the 2 body pieces and, using an embroidery needle threaded with 1 strand of chocolate brown embroidery floss, sew together using a small, neat overstitch. Leave the neck open and lightly pad the body with a little toy stuffing before overstitching the gap closed.

7 Position the head so that it overlaps the body. Use an embroidery needle and 1 strand of light brown floss to stitch the body and head together, using a small, neat overstitch and sewing through all 4 layers of felt. Try to place the new stitches over the earlier overstitching for a neat finish.

8 For the final touches to Curly Ram, stick on his woolly hair with a dot of craft glue. Thread the bell, if using, on a double strand of orange embroidery floss. Tie around his neck, knotting neatly at the back.

Samurai Cat

This little cat started out as a ninja, swathed in black for covert operations under the cloak of darkness, but somehow his accessories gradually grew brighter…So now he is a samurai cat in informal wear, with a hat modeled on the traditional straw versions worn by Japanese farmers.

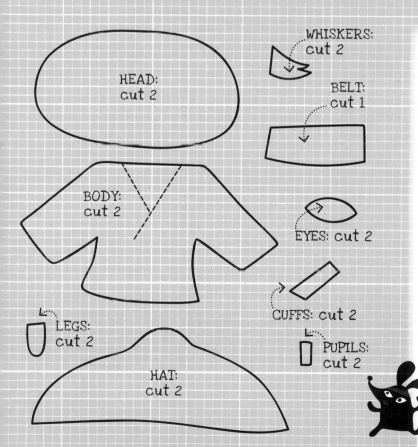

HEAD: cut 2

WHISKERS: cut 2

BELT: cut 1

BODY: cut 2

EYES: cut 2

LEGS: cut 2

CUFFS: cut 2

PUPILS: cut 2

HAT: cut 2

YOU WILL NEED

- ★ 6-inch (15-cm) square of black felt
- ★ 6-inch (15-cm) square of beige felt
- ★ 4-inch (10-cm) square of yellow felt
- ★ Small scraps of red and white felt
- ★ Embroidery floss in black, beige, yellow, and red
- ★ Tiny quantity of toy stuffing
- ★ Embroidery needle
- ★ Scissors
- ★ Pencil
- ★ Tracing paper
- ★ Craft glue
- ★ Toothpick or matchstick

To make Samurai Cat

1 Trace off the pattern pieces on page 57 onto tracing paper and cut them out to make templates. Cut 2 pieces each for the body, legs, and pupils from the black felt; 2 pieces each for the head and whiskers from the beige felt; 2 pieces for the hat from the yellow felt; 1 piece for the belt and 2 for the cuffs from the red felt; and 2 eyes from the white felt. Stick the eyes in place with a little craft glue, checking against the photograph to position correctly. Glue a pupil in the center of each eye.

2 Thread an embroidery needle with 2 strands of black embroidery floss and embroider the nose and mouth—2 straight stitches in a downward "V" shape for the mouth, then 1 vertical straight stitch and 3 horizontal straight stitches in an inverted triangle for the nose. Make the fringe with 3 slightly angled long straight stitches, and loosen them a little in a curve; fasten off the thread at the back. Use a dot of glue to keep the curved shape of the fringe in place.

3 Use a little craft glue to stick the whiskers in place on one side of the second face shape. Align the head pieces, right sides out. Thread the embroidery needle with 1 strand of beige floss, and sew together using a small, neat overstitch. Leave a gap at the neck (don't fasten off the thread) and pad the head with a tiny amount of toy stuffing, using a toothpick or matchstick to distribute it evenly. Overstitch the gap closed.

4 Using 2 strands of yellow floss, backstitch 3 evenly spaced, slightly curving lines across one of the hat pieces. Fasten off the thread. Now using 1 strand of yellow floss, sew the front and back of the hat together along the top using a small, neat overstitch. Slide the hat onto the head and overstitch in place; feed in minute pieces of toy stuffing as you stitch, to pad the hat.

5 Glue the legs in place on the back of 1 of the body pieces. Thread the needle with 2 strands of red floss and embroider the closure detail on the front of the body in chain stitch, following the stitching lines shown on the template.

6 Align the 2 body pieces, right sides out. Use 1 strand of black floss to sew together, using a small, neat overstitch. Leave the neck open (don't fasten off the thread) and pad the body lightly with toy stuffing, and distribute it evenly before stitching the gap closed.

7 Glue the belt and cuffs in place on the front of the body. Using 2 strands of black floss, position 2 horizontal stripes of floss across the belt and a single one around each sleeve; stitch in place at either end at the back of the body.

8 Position the head so that it slightly overlaps the body. Using 1 strand of beige floss, sew the head and body together using a small, neat overstitch. Try to place the new stitches over the existing ones for a neat finish.

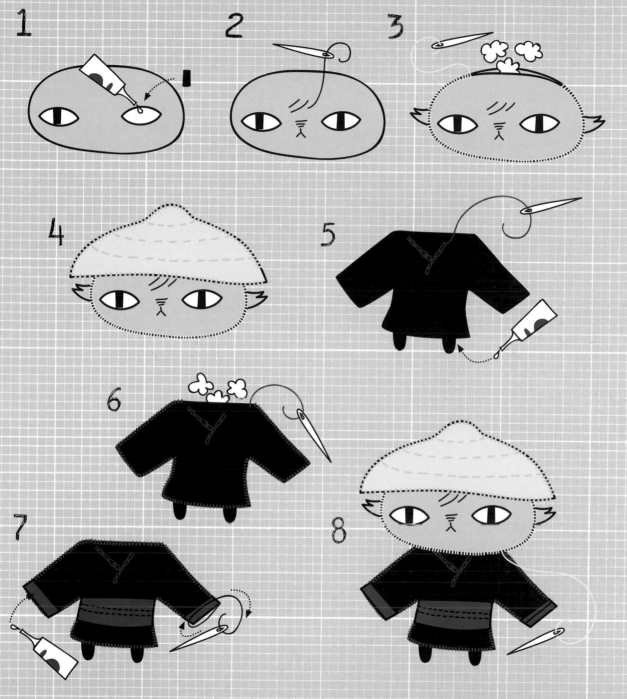

Mummy Cat

The Ancient Egyptians worshipped cats and mummified their bodies. Mummy Cat has clearly strayed in from some similarly antique culture: she's a little otherworldly, and she's fraying just a bit around the edges, but her sweet face and wide, innocent eyes let us know that the intentions of this tiny tomb dweller are entirely benign.

BODY:
cut 2

TAIL:
cut 1

YOU WILL NEED

★ 4-inch (10-cm) square of white felt

★ A small roll of cotton first-aid bandage. You'll need a strip about 1 yard (91 cm) long and ½ inch (1.3 cm) wide

★ Embroidery floss in black and white

★ Tiny quantity of toy stuffing

★ Embroidery needle

★ Scissors

★ Pencil

★ Tracing paper

★ Craft glue

★ Toothpick or matchstick

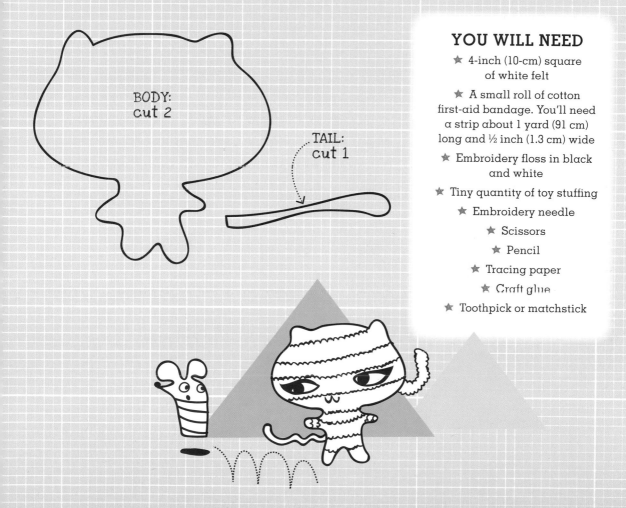

To make Mummy Cat

1 Trace off the pattern pieces on page 61 onto tracing paper and cut out to make templates. Use to cut out 2 pieces each for the body and 1 piece for the tail from the white felt.

2 Cut a long strip of bandage from the roll, about 1 yard long and ½ inch wide. Take 1 of the body pieces, and use a dot of craft glue to stick one end of the bandage in from the edge at the top of the head.

3 Gently and carefully wind the bandage around the entire body piece in overlapping spirals, flattening it with your fingers as you wind for a neat finish. When you reach the feet, cut off the end of the bandage, leaving about ½ inch (1.3cm) to fold to the wrong side; glue the last ½ inch (1.3cm) neatly in place on the wrong side of the body front with a dot of craft glue.

4 Thread an embroidery needle with 2 strands of black embroidery floss and make the mouth with 2 little joined "V"s of backstitch (4 stitches in all).

5 Stitch the eyes, again using 2 strands of black embroidery floss. The outline for each eye is almond-shaped and sewn in backstitch— 4 stitches each for the top and bottom line of the eye. Now stitch the pupils, using single long vertical straight stitches positioned very close together to make solid black squares (this is called "satin stitch").

6 Help the Mummy Cat to "unravel" a little by cutting a tiny strip from the remaining bandage and sticking it to the wrong side of the bandaged body piece with a little glue, so that it hangs out loosely from the cheek. Glue the tail in position, too.

7 Align the 2 body pieces, right sides out. Thread the embroidery needle with 1 strand of white embroidery floss and sew the body together using a small, neat overstitch. Leave the top of the head open and lightly pad the body with toy stuffing, using a toothpick or matchstick to distribute the padding evenly. Overstitch the gap closed.

8 Brush the tip of a toothpick or matchstick dipped sparingly in craft glue along the raw edges of the bandages on the front of the Mummy Cat to prevent them from fraying. Leave the Mummy cat propped up against a flat surface until the glue is completely dry.

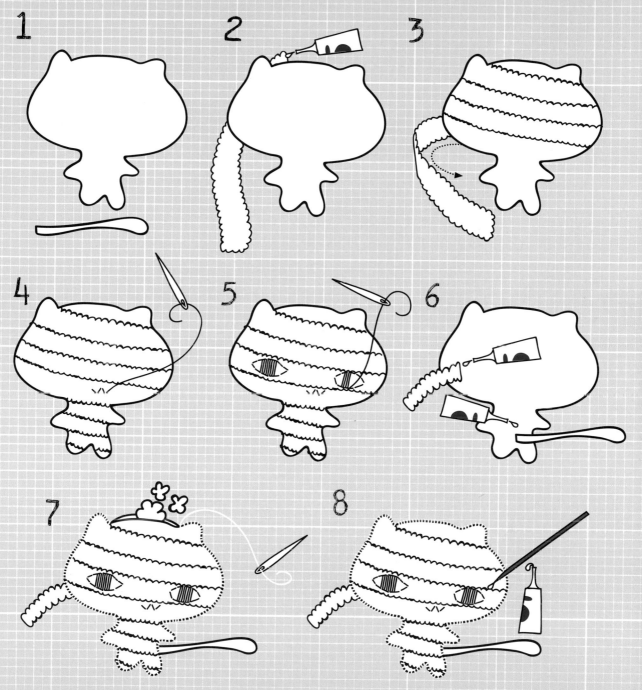

Retro Alien

There's nothing modern about this Retro Alien: he has vivid green skin, an oversize head, elliptical eyes, and gleaming bead "monitors" ornamenting his forehead. Could this be your favorite Martian? And should you suspect some elaborate Roswell-style hoax, there's a little picture of his home planet helpfully rendered on the front of his body.

YOU WILL NEED

- ★ 6-inch (15-cm) square of bright green felt
- ★ Small scraps of black and blue felt
- ★ Embroidery floss in white, black, and bright green
- ★ 11 tiny metallic yellow beads
- ★ Tiny quantity of toy stuffing
- ★ Embroidery needle
- ★ Beading needle
- ★ Scissors
- ★ Pencil
- ★ Tracing paper
- ★ Craft glue
- ★ Toothpick or matchstick

HEAD:
cut 2

EYES:
cut 2

ARMS:
cut 2

BODY:
cut 2

PLANET:
cut 1

To make Retro Alien

1 Trace off the pattern pieces on page 65 onto tracing paper and cut out to make templates. Use to cut 2 pieces each for the body and the head from the green felt, 2 pieces each for the eyes and arms from the black felt, and 1 circle for Retro Alien's planet badge from the blue felt. Use a little craft glue to stick the eyes in a slanting position on the front of one of the head pieces.

2 Thread an embroidery needle with 2 strands of white embroidery floss and embroider a pupil in the center of each eye using a double French knot. Use 2 strands of black embroidery floss to embroider the mouth, using a double French knot and placing it slightly off center and toward the bottom of Retro Alien's face.

3 Thread a beading needle with 1 strand of bright green embroidery floss and sew 2 rows of beads onto Retro Alien's head, adding them one by one in straight vertical lines and working directly up the face from the eyes to the top of the head (see page 7 for using beads).

4 Keep the embroidery needle threaded with 1 strand of bright green embroidery floss. Align the two head pieces, right sides out, and sew together using a small, neat overstitch. Leave a space at the base of the head (don't fasten off the thread) and lightly pad the head with a tiny quantity of toy stuffing, using a toothpick or matchstick to distribute evenly. Overstitch the gap closed.

5 Take one of the body pieces and use a tiny amount of craft glue to stick the blue felt planet shape on the center front. Thread an embroidery needle with 2 strands of black embroidery floss and stitch the ring around the planet with 3 long straight stitches. If necessary, put a tiny touch of glue on the point of a toothpick or matchstick and dab on very carefully in a couple of places to hold the curve of the ring stitches in place.

6 Take the other body piece and stick the two arms in position on either side (this is the wrong side).

7 Align the 2 body pieces, right sides out, and use a needle threaded with one strand of bright green floss to overstitch the pieces together. Leave the neck open and fill your alien with a tiny amount of toy stuffing. When it is evenly arranged, stitch the opening shut.

8 Position the head so that it overlaps the body. Using an embroidery needle and 1 strand of bright green embroidery floss, overstitch the head and body together, stitching through all 4 layers of felt. Try to place the new stitches over the earlier ones for a neat finish.

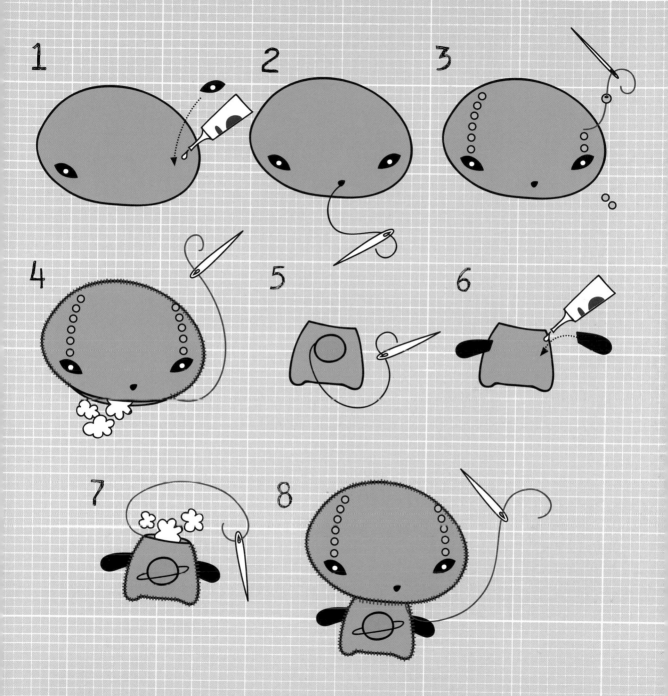

Pirate Mouse

A pretty color scheme and the glitter of a golden bandolier belt belie Pirate Mouse's true role: bold buccaneer ready to hold to ransom any other feltie for a rich reward. She may not have a parrot on her shoulder, but she's daring enough to make her living in an unorthodox way, and she has the eye patch to prove it.

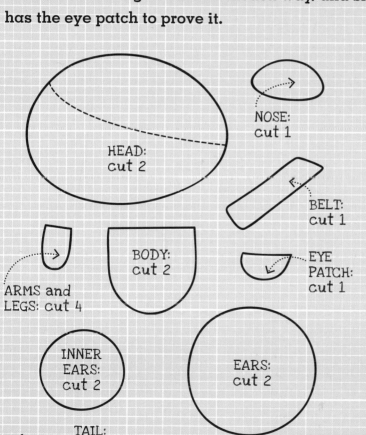

NOSE: cut 1

HEAD: cut 2

BELT: cut 1

ARMS and LEGS: cut 4

BODY: cut 2

EYE PATCH: cut 1

INNER EARS: cut 2

EARS: cut 2

TAIL: cut 1

YOU WILL NEED

- ★ 6-inch (15-cm) square of lilac felt
- ★ Small scraps of lemon yellow, black, and brown felt
- ★ Scrap of lilac felt or lemon yellow yarn and crochet hook (if you want to crochet the tail)
- ★ Embroidery floss in black, lilac, and brown
- ★ 1 dark metallic bead, about ⅛ inch (3 cm) in diameter
- ★ 8 gold bugle beads
- ★ Tiny quantity of toy stuffing
- ★ Embroidery needle
- ★ Beading needle
- ★ Scissors
- ★ Pencil
- ★ Tracing paper
- ★ Craft glue
- ★ Toothpick or matchstick

To make Pirate Mouse

1 Trace off the pattern pieces on page 69 onto tracing paper and cut out to make templates. Use to cut out 2 head, 2 body, and 2 ear pieces from the lilac felt; 4 arm and leg shapes, 1 nose, and 2 inner ear pieces from the lemon yellow felt; 1 eye patch from the black felt; and 1 bandolier belt from the brown felt. You can choose to either crochet Pirate Mouse's tail or cut it out from lilac felt using the template to cut the pattern piece.

2 Use a dot of craft glue to stick the nose onto one of the face pieces. Thread an embroidery needle with two strands of black embroidery floss and embroider the nose by working 2 straight stitches arranged in a "T" shape. Embroider a curving line above the nose using backstitch. This is the string for the eye patch.

3 Thread a beading needle with 1 strand of black embroidery floss and sew the dark metallic bead in place on the face to make Pirate Mouse's right eye. Use craft glue to stick the eye patch in place on its embroidered "string."

4 Now use a little craft glue to stick the inner ears in place, then glue the ears onto the head piece. Thread an embroidery needle with 1 strand of lilac embroidery floss, align the 2 head pieces, right sides out, and sew together with a small, neat overstitch. Leave a small gap open along the lower edge of the head (don't fasten off the thread) and pad the head evenly with a tiny amount of toy stuffing. Overstitch the gap closed.

5 Thread a beading needle with 1 strand of brown embroidery floss and sew the bugle beads onto the belt. Leave a gap somewhere in the line of "bullets" to show that some ammunition has already been used. When the beads are sewn in place, fasten off the thread, and glue the belt onto the body at an angle.

6 Take the second body piece and use a little craft glue to stick the arms and legs onto the wrong side. To make a crochet tail, use the lemon yellow yarn to crochet a chain 20 stitches long. Otherwise, use the felt tail cut from the template. Carefully cut a tiny slit in the body (back piece) and feed through the base of the tail (just enough so that you can secure it firmly). Use a little craft glue to fix in place on the wrong side.

7 Align the 2 body pieces, right sides out. Thread an embroidery needle with 1 strand of lilac embroidery floss and sew the body pieces together using a small, neat overstitch. Leave a small gap open at the neck area (don't fasten off the thread) and fill the body with a small amount of toy stuffing. Pad the body evenly, then overstitch the gap closed.

8 Position the head so that it overlaps the body. Using an embroidery needle and 1 strand of lilac embroidery floss, overstitch the head and body together, stitching through all 4 layers of felt. Try to place the new stitches over the earlier ones for a neat finish.

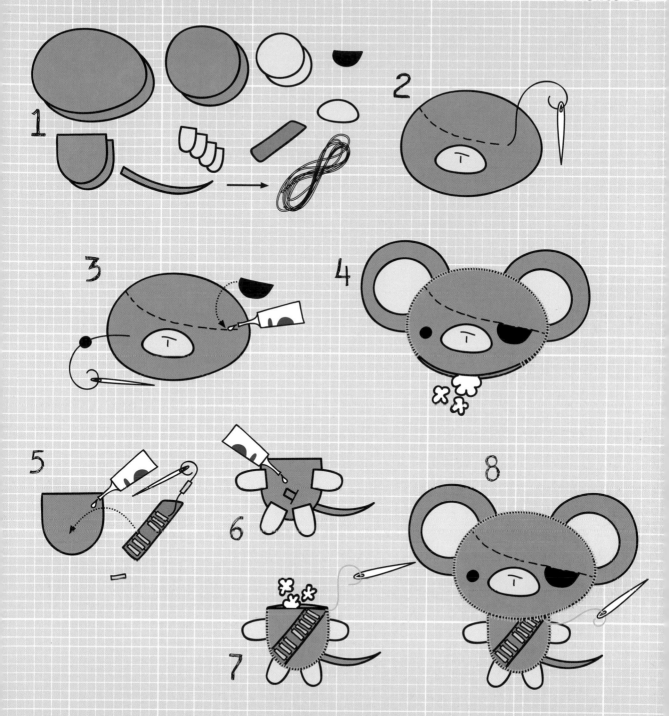

Vivid Squirrel

This vibrant, brightly colored squirrel has already taken possession of an enviably large acorn, but her eyes are cast upward to see if she can catch sight of another. If she's going to settle in for a peaceful hibernation, she'll need all the solid fuel she can find to keep her warm and snug through the winter.

YOU WILL NEED

- ★ 6-inch (15-cm) square of yellow felt
- ★ Small scraps of chocolate brown, black, tan, and pale brown felt
- ★ Embroidery floss in black, white, yellow, and tan
- ★ Tiny quantity of toy stuffing
- ★ Embroidery needle
- ★ Scissors
- ★ Pencil
- ★ Disappearing marking pen
- ★ Tracing paper
- ★ Craft glue
- ★ Toothpick or matchstick

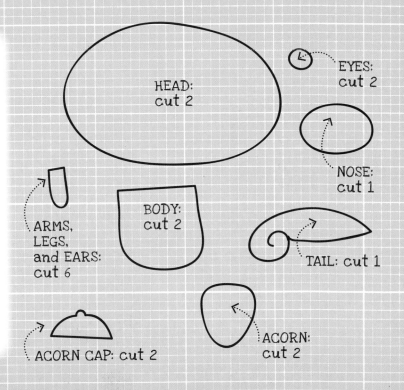

HEAD: cut 2

EYES: cut 2

NOSE: cut 1

ARMS, LEGS, and EARS: cut 6

BODY: cut 2

TAIL: cut 1

ACORN CAP: cut 2

ACORN: cut 2

To make Vivid Squirrel

1 Trace off the pattern pieces on page 72 onto tracing paper and cut out to make templates. Cut out 2 pieces each for the head and body from the yellow felt; 1 piece each for the nose and tail, plus 6 identical pieces for the arms, legs, and ears, from the chocolate brown felt; 2 eyes from the black felt; 2 pieces for the acorn from the tan felt; and 2 pieces for the acorn cap from the pale brown felt. Take one of the head pieces and use tiny dots of craft glue to stick the eyes in place. Check against the photograph to position them correctly.

2 Thread an embroidery needle with 2 strands of black embroidery floss and embroider the features: the eyelashes are made with 2 straight stitches extending from the outer edge of each eye; the line up to the nose is a row of 4 backstitches; and the mouth is a single short straight stitch made at a slight angle to give Vivid Squirrel her wry expression. Rethread the needle with 4 strands of white embroidery floss and add pupils to the eyes by working a triple French knot in the center of each one.

3 Use a little craft glue to stick the ears in position on the wrong side of the second head piece. Align the 2 head pieces, right sides out.

4 Using an embroidery needle and 1 strand of yellow floss, sew together using a small, neat overstitch. Leave a small gap along the lower edge and evenly pad the head with a small amount of toy stuffing. Overstitch the gap closed.

5 Use a little craft glue to stick the nose in position on the upper part of the head. Thread an embroidery needle with 2 strands of black embroidery floss. Embroider 2 small straight stitches in a "T"shape to make the nostrils.

6 Glue Vivid Squirrel's arms and legs in position on the wrong side of one body piece. Cut the full curve shown on the template into the tail piece, turn the outer end inward, and stick in place with a tiny dot of glue to give the tail a slight curl at the end.

7 Align the 2 body pieces, right sides out. Using an embroidery needle and 1 strand of yellow embroidery floss, sew together using a small, neat overstitch. Leave open at the neck and lightly pad the body with a tiny amount of toy stuffing. Overstitch the gap closed.

8 Position the head so that it overlaps the body. Using an embroidery needle and 1 strand of yellow embroidery floss, overstitch the body and head together, stitching through all 4 layers of felt. Try to place the new stitches over the earlier overstitching for a neat finish.

9 Finally, make the acorn. Using the pale brown embroidery floss, overstitch the 2 main acorn pieces together, leaving open at the top. Lightly pad with a little toy stuffing. Overstitch the gap closed. Glue the 2 acorn cap pieces in place, one on each side of the top of the acorn.

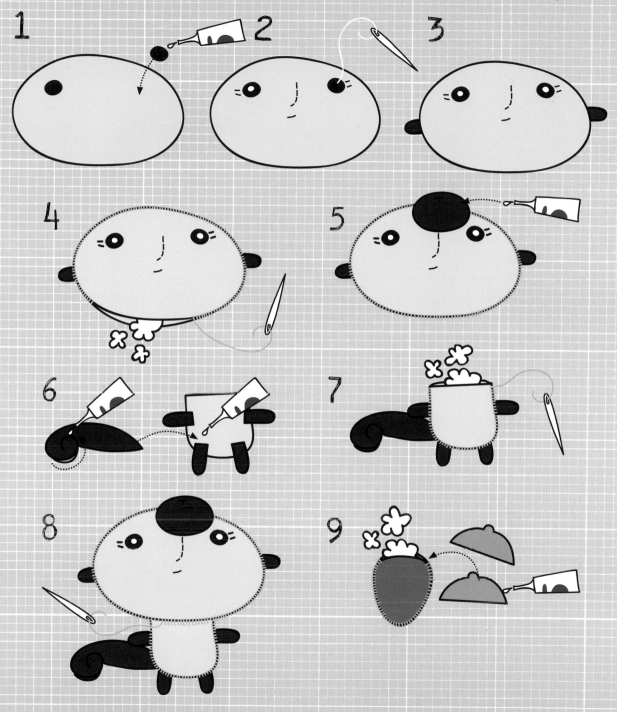

Hoodie Wolf

In the fairy tale, the wolf gobbles up Red Riding Hood and her grandmother. Here, although he's already appropriated the heroine's cape, he's not yet started on the delicious snack—a toothsome pie and a baguette—in the basket. Perhaps when he's eaten them he'll feel too full to eat any humans and the tale will have a happy ending.

YOU WILL NEED

- ★ 6-inch (15-cm) square of red felt
- ★ 4-inch (10-cm) square of gray felt
- ★ 3-inch (7.5-cm) square of brown felt
- ★ Small scraps of beige and white felt
- ★ Embroidery floss in black, white, red, brown, and beige
- ★ 2 tiny black beads
- ★ Tiny quantity of toy stuffing
- ★ Embroidery needle
- ★ Beading needle
- ★ Scissors
- ★ Pencil
- ★ Tracing paper
- ★ Craft glue
- ★ Toothpick or matchstick

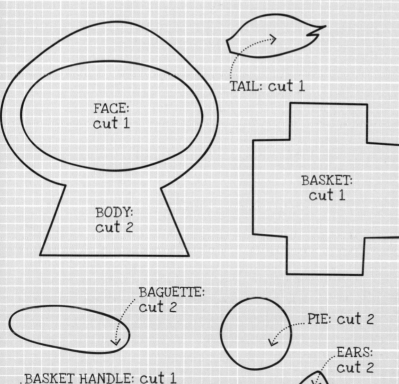

FACE: cut 1

TAIL: cut 1

BODY: cut 2

BASKET: cut 1

BAGUETTE: cut 2

PIE: cut 2

EARS: cut 2

BASKET HANDLE: cut 1

To make Hoodie Wolf

1 Trace off the pattern pieces on page 77 onto tracing paper and cut out to make templates. Use to cut out the pieces as follows: 2 pieces each for the body from the red felt, 2 pieces for the ears and 1 each for the tail and face from the gray felt. Cut out 1 piece for the basket body and 1 for the handle from the brown felt, 2 pieces for the baguette and 1 piece for the pie back from the beige felt, 1 piece for the top from the white felt.

2 Thread an embroidery needle with 2 strands of black embroidery floss and embroider the nose in a "T" shape, using a short straight horizontal stitch at the top and a much longer straight vertical stitch centered underneath it. Next, embroider the mouth, a curving line of backstitch on either side of the nose, and 8 tooth shapes underneath, each made from a "V" of 2 straight stitches.

3 Thread a beading needle with 1 strand of black embroidery floss and sew Hoodie Wolf's 2 bead eyes in position on the face. Now thread an embroidery needle with 2 strands of white embroidery floss and stitch French knots to fill in the teeth——this gives the mouth some volume and the wolf a voracious white grin.

4 Use a little craft glue to stick the face onto one of the body pieces. Using 2 strands of black embroidery floss, stitch 2 French knots for the "buttons" on the front of the cape. Check against the photograph to position correctly.

5 Take 1 strand of black embroidery floss and tie a bow in it. Secure in place above the buttons, using an embroidery needle, black floss, and a couple of tiny straight stitches.

6 Glue the ears and the tail onto the wrong side of the second body piece. Align both body pieces, right sides out. Using an embroidery needle and 1 strand of red embroidery floss, sew together with a small, neat overstitch. Leave a small gap along the top of the head and lightly pad the body with stuffing, using a toothpick or matchstick to help you to get the padding even. Overstitch the gap closed.

7 To make the basket, thread an embroidery needle with 2 strands of brown embroidery floss and stitch together the basket sides at each of the 4 corners to make a shallow tray shape. Overstitch around the top edge of the basket. Use craft glue to stick the handle inside each of the long sides, so that it makes a loop.

8 To make the baguette, stitch both pieces together using an embroidery needle and 1 strand of beige embroidery floss. Push in wisps of stuffing as you sew. To make the pie, embroider three French knots with 2 strands of red embroidery floss on the white pie top, to look like cherries. Overstitch the pie and bottom together, using 1 strand of beige embroidery floss and pushing in wisps of stuffing as you sew. Arrange both pie and baguette attractively in the basket.

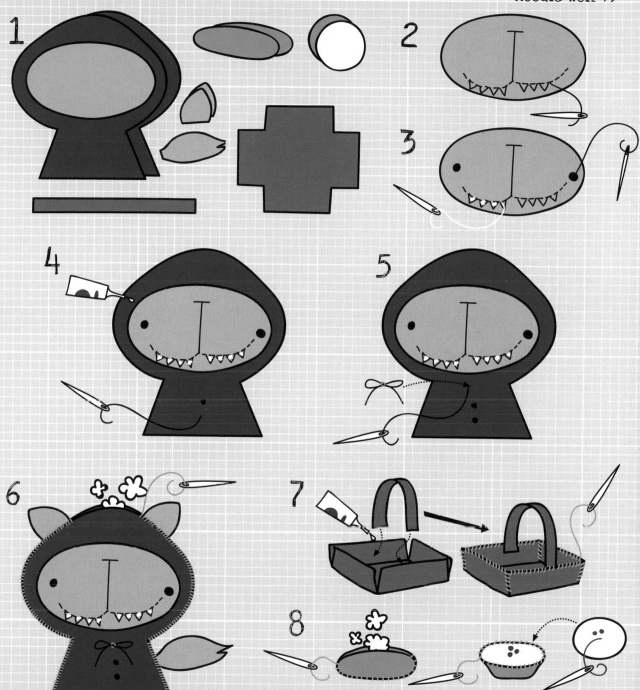

Index